JN060338

Founders

Blake Roney

Sandie Tillotson

Steven Lund

Nedra Roney

Advisory Board Member

Paul Cox

TE Distributor

Tamako Kishimoto

People whom I quoted

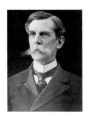
Oliver Wendell Holmes

Walt Disney

Thomas Jefferson

Yozan Uesugi

Mark Twain

Dale Carnegie

Albert Einstein

Masayuki Kishimoto
Written Works

2002	"Nafanua" (Goldman Environmental Prize winner, Dr. Paul Cox) translation and publishing, book selected by the Japan Library Association
2007	published "50th anniversary magazine; University of the Ryukyus"
2015	Published "We Live on a Small Blue Planet: Towards Establishing a Global Government"
2017	Published "Global Government 2017: Making Global Citizen Education Mandatory"
2019	Published "Global Government 2017" (English version of the above) Published "Philanthropy from the Beyond: Adopting a Culture of Higher Education & Changing the World"
2020	Published "Philanthropy from the Beyond: Adopting a Culture of Higher Education & Changing the World" (English version of "Philanthropy from the Beyond")
2022	Published "Forwarding Peace Road: Globalization and the Path to World Peace"
2022	Published "Analects of the Founders' Quotes and Sayings"
2023	Slated to publish "Forwarding Peace Road" (English version of "Forwarding Peace Road")
2023	Slated to publish "The Day Borders Disappear"
2023	Slated to publish "The Day Borders Disappear" (English version of "The Day Borders Disappear")

English Version

English Version   English Version   English Version

All royalties from books will be donated to the relief of child hunger in the poorest countries, such as in Africa, Japan, and donated to the Kishimoto Family Foundation Action Fund.

Analects of the Founders' Quotes, Sayings, & Other Heartfelt Words

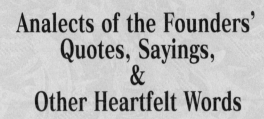

by Masayuki Kishimoto
Founder of the Kishimoto Family Foundation

文芸社

CONTENTS

Preface

My experience meeting the founder and president Blake Roney was truly once in a lifetime. That's because it completely changed life for me and my wife. It was when I was 54 years old. It was around that same time that I met Senior Vice President Sandie Tillotson and Vice President and Managing Director Steven Lund.

It was also around the same time that my wife and I met Dr. Paul Cox, the founder of the Seacology Foundation, who we now respect as our lifelong mentor. These were truly fateful encounters.

The first face-to-face meetings with President Roney and Dr. Cox were both at lectures that were extremely astounding. The title of President Roney's lecture was "Corporate Missions and Social Responsibility." I felt a number of what seemed like strong electrical shocks while listening to the lecture. The memory is still deeply ingrained in my mind.

As I immersed myself in the afterglow of the lecture, I felt an urge to meet them and rushed to the waiting room behind the stage immediately after the lecture. That was when my self-awakening began.

My title on my business card at that time was "Marketing Technician." I was secretly very proud of that title.

However, I was shocked by their lectures. For the first time, I realized that my marketing efforts were biased towards balancing profits and losses. I felt miserable at my immaturity. I was caught up in the mistaken marketing common sense and customary profit-seeking of the time. That realization acted as a turning point in my life.

Since then, I have come to sincerely respect both of them as lifelong mentors. The more I listened to their lectures, the more I felt my senses of self, humanity, values, society, and worldview become elevated and my heart lifted. Both of them have genuine, warm hearts.

Deep down inside, everyone wants to serve others and be useful in society. However, whether we can find opportunities to be useful is the real problem. Nu Skin offers those opportunities to many people in 52 countries around the world.

In 1984, Blake Roney, Nedra Roney, Sandie Tillotson, and Steven Lund founded Nu Skin Enterprises (NSE) in Provo, Utah, USA. President Roney invested $5,000 from his own savings as starting capital. They rented a private garage and opened business. With the groundbreaking product philosophy of "All of the Good, None of the Bad," they started manufacturing and selling beauty products.

In 1993, the company started operations as Nu Skin Japan in the seventh-largest market in the world. Nu Skin was listed on the New York Stock Exchange in 1996. As of 2021, it has expanded its business in 52 countries around the world and has about 1.56 million members, about 825,000 active independent distributors, total annual sales of approximately $2.7 billion, and approximately 5,000 employees. Today, it has become one of the world's largest direct selling companies.

So, I was inspired to ask why Nu Skin has grown into a leading company in the world at such an astounding rate, doing so in one generation, and where it will head now. At the time of its establishment, highly capable PCs and digital technologies had not been developed like they are today.

On the contrary, the online direct sales industry was not properly understood by the general public around the world. We couldn't even imagine the astronomical sales records of the Big Four (GAFA) in recent years. But all over the world, the uncommon sense of the past changes to the common sense of the present.

As I frequently came to hear President Roney's words,

"strangely enough, our company has developed further the more we have served others" in his lectures, I wished to understand what he meant by "strangely enough."

So, I came up with a hypothesis. The hypothesis is that the main reason for the company's rapid development is their founding spirit of "Force for Good," meaning to serve others and contribute to society. Since its founding, Nu Skin has been an advocate of the noble "Force for Good" corporate philosophy. The corporate philosophy is to "be a force to enrich people both physically and spiritually."

In order to prove that hypothesis, I worked on searching, examining, and evaluating the founders' quotes, adages, and sayings. The verification and evaluation were based on the classification model (citations) set by the founder Blake Roney and on the Explanatory Notes of this book.

Major citations include: Inspirational, Motivational, Positive, Wisdom, Freedom, Knowledge, Leadership, Friendship, Dream, Success, Life, Love, and Happiness.

To my surprise, the spirit of being a Force for Good existed in the minds of the founders even before the company was founded. To give an analogy, the season had already come and the flowers had blossomed. The moment I discovered this, I was so deeply impressed that it is difficult to describe.

Many organizations in Japan and overseas have commended Nu Skin's "practical achievements of serving others and contributing to society." Even simply listing the instances of such requires many pages.

Cases of Nu Skin's "leading examples" of charitable acts have, one after the other, been reported by domestic and foreign public media under headlines such as "Social Service Company," "Hunger Relief Company," "Charity Company," "High Distributor Pay Company," "Billionaires' Mass Production Company," "Moving, Fantastic Company," "Cutting Edge Tech Development Company," and "Top Company to Join."

At the same time, they have thoroughly tightened discipline within the company and have taken appropriate measures against violators of their terms and the law. There are also many cases of distributors' contracts being terminated and employees being dismissed.

Corporate education, which aims to reform awareness to improve corporate and social order, is continuously promoted on a global scale. As a part of this, they are also enthusiastic about ideological education for the coexistence and co-prosperity of all people. Such corporate activities will also undoubtedly promote collective awareness reform among global citizens who are longing for lasting peace in the world.

Within "historical events, idioms, adages quotes, and sayings" lies the immortal wisdom that humanity has cultivated over many years. It is the wisdom to improve people's way of thinking. It also gives us the hope and courage to live. There is nothing in this world that surpasses the joy of finding "purpose" in life.

First of all, "historical events" are full of stories that distill, essentialize, enliven, and release the fragrance of the rising and falling of humanity from all times and places.

"Idioms" spell out the purpose of life and the dignity of ways of living are written in elegant stanzas and with fine rhythm. Idioms also stimulate deep thoughts one after another, penetrating deep into the heart. Finally, they make people into "thinkers who act."

"Sayings" crystallize and cosmologize the myriad thoughts of man. They spell out man's thoughts as noble admonitions and exhortations. They truly mimic the greatness of literature, which transcends time, and captivate people's hearts.

"Quotes" contain the permeation of sentiments, brewing and selection of thought, and the breath of the meaning of life, which all flow from the rhythm and words thereof. They are not vulgar, meaningless hearsay or exaggerations.

The historical events, idioms, adages, quotes, and sayings of all times and places give constant reprimands and encouragement to people while shining the light of hope in the direction in which future human civilization should head.

"Idioms," which have long collaborated with historical events, will not oxidize or deteriorate in the long term, even after undergoing the transformation of values over time. They instruct us to not let man's "way of thinking" deviate from its fundamental axis, despite changes in era and social order.

The "paradigm shifts (changes in thought)" sought after by changes in era must be brought about before stepping on the accelerator that progresses us toward future ideals. If we miss that timing, the course of human progress will be disrupted, leading to catastrophic opposition, conflict, and killing. In the worst case, it will even lead to the "destruction of mankind." In our time where nuclear proliferation is escalating, humanity must never let our intuition for foreseeing global crisis be dulled.

If mankind were to be able to make the appropriate "paradigm shift" to fill the "gap between the ideal and reality" in a timely manner, nobody in the human world would say "impossible" anymore. In other words, the "beautiful traditions" of human historical events can be considered the result of "paradigm shift sustainability."

"Eternal sayings" that transcend time will serve as a guide for modern people who live in today's world to learn the purpose for living and rational thinking. Feeling one's purpose for living is proof of progress down the road of life. Eternal sayings and adages are the precious "heritage of knowledge" that our predecessors left to their posterity.

Eternal sayings that transcend time will act as a "motto" for life for those who live in the present day. When exploring the future of our way of living, our imaginations and inspirations will help us create an ideal image of future society. Inspirational thought stimulation helps improve people's knowledge and helps people acquire the habit of thinking in an elaborate manner.

Words and thoughts are two sides of the same coin. The two cannot be separated. People think with words, and thought requires careful selection of words. That is to say, when words change, our thoughts change, and when our thoughts change, the world in which we live changes. By extension, the world changes, and even the fate of people changes.

By thoroughly exploring the meaning of adages, we power the driving force that brings about the ultimate dream of humanity, "lasting world peace." In other words, as human intellect, discernment, foresight, and sense of direction are refined, more people will desire the establishment of a "global central government" that will never allow wars of atrocity and meaningless slaughter.

In other words, we, humanity, are approaching our ultimate goal step by step. When I think about it, my heart races, and I can hear my heart palpitate.

Dreams are sought through action. What we seek with action is always fulfilled. Optimism is better than pessimism. In other words, the truth is self-evident that positive thinking outweighs negative thinking.

Let us learn from historical events, idioms, adages, quotes, and sayings from all times and places to enrich our lives.

Explanatory Notes

• What is the original source of the idioms, adages, and quotes that I want to reference? This is a difficult question. There are many dictionaries in the world. Among them, the number of types of dictionaries for idioms, adages, quotes, and sayings is on another level. Therefore, many are listed as "Source: Unknown." It is estimated that many of the sources date back to the Bible and other scripture.

• The authors of many idioms, adages, quotes, and sayings are unknown. Or perhaps they do not exist. There are many similar works and "counterfeits," and they may have multiple authors. Over long years, many have become familiar with and rewritten various sayings and adages. These now serve as admonitions and exhortations to the public and have become the wisdom of life. In turn, they have begun to take an important role as a compass showing the way for human civilization.

• This book is mainly composed of "heartfelt quotes, adages, and sayings" from the Nu Skin Enterprises (NSE) founders, President and Chairman Blake Roney, Senior Vice President Sandie Tillotson, and Vice President and Managing Director Steven Lund. I also added analogous sayings and related quotes from Dr. Paul Alan Cox and top Nu Skin distributors, whom I and my wife regard as lifelong mentors.

- The historical events, idioms, quotes, and sayings compiled in this book have been searched out from various "Source:" materials before being subject to editorial supervision. However, "Source:" does not necessarily mean the "original source." It is almost impossible to prove original sources except for historical events.

- I endeavored to collect sayings, adages, and quotes that I hoped would inspire even just one more reader to make them their motto. This is because I think they reveal the sublime and the savage of humanity.

- The sayings and quotes included in this book are sourced from Nu Skin Enterprises (NSE) publications, brochures, training texts, newsletters, distributor-produced VTRs, cassette tapes, "The Success Formula: Today's Quotes," websites, founders' training reports, orientation materials, lecturers' speech scripts, Nu Skin Japan (hereinafter; NSJ) Founders' Quotes: "This Month's Words" Leading to Success, "AZ Quotes: Founders," distributor notes, idiom dictionaries, social media, etc.

- Most of the idioms, adages, sayings, and quotes cited around the world are thought to have roots in numerous religious and sectarian texts as their original source. Many of them date back to the divine age of Genesis or are derived from ancient texts. Therefore, it is considered extremely difficult to build a case for "copyright/right to cite" from a legal standpoint. Therefore, the sources described in this book cannot be called the "original."

- It must be said that due to the ambiguous and mutable nature of terms, the recency and antiquatedness of regional and ethnic languages, the ease of rewriting, the diversity of ethnic cultures, the uniqueness of the interpretation of terms, the varying nature of commonly used terms across epochs, etc., the "lack of clarity of short phrases" of the idioms, sayings, adages, and quotes cited all over the world is inevitable.

- In short, it is thought that asserting the "right to cite" around the world for the "short phrases" of idioms, adages, sayings, and quotes is not consistent with the academic logic of linguistics and logic. Therefore, I believe that the historical events, idioms, sayings, and adages from all times and places should be considered as a world cultural heritage shared by all mankind. I truly believe so.

- Wikipedia, YouTube, other social media platforms, a wide variety of search apps, distributor personal notes, public media excerpts, websites, and more have become one of the most popular means of communication in the current world of social media.

- I hope this serves as a springboard for everyone to become self-disciplined, while familiarizing themselves with the historical events, idioms, adages, and quotes left by the sages of all times and places. The joy of self-development makes people into "experts." As the number of experts increase, social change accelerates.

Founders' Sayings, Adages, and Quotes

Quotes and Sayings of Blake Roney

1

"The journey will never be easy, smooth sailing, but it will be always worth it to the extreme."

Source: NSE publications

2

Similar quote: "We must sail sometimes with wind and sometimes against to it — but we must sail, and not drift, nor lie at anchor." (Oliver Wendell Holmes)

Source: NSE publications

3

"Becoming A Force for Good"

Source: Nu Skin Newsletter

4

Explanatory quote: "Distilling the company values into a single moniker, he coined the phrase 'force for good.' Soon, this idea grew into an official Nu Skin initiative known as the Nu Skin Force for Good Foundation."

Source: NSE publications

5

"As long as we continue to be a force for good in the world, improving people's lives through innovative products and unmatched opportunities, and as long as we continue to provide the critical, comprehensive support required by our amazing, gifted distributor force, nothing will stop us."

Source: NSE publications

Compiler's Note: This is the essence of Nu Skin's spirit and culture. It is the greatest pleasure to serve others and contribute to society. Also, the philosophy of "coexistence and co-prosperity" is a universal and unchanging value in human society. A corresponding reward system was also created.

6

Analogous quote: "Since the beginning of our founding, we have been working to become a Force for Good in the world. Nourish the Children gives malnourished and starving children a breath of life. There is nothing better than the on-site implementation of Force for Good."

Source: NSE publications and brochures

7

"Many who discover the company through the products, or the opportunity may never have heard of the Nu Skin Force for Good Foundation, but they sense it. They know that something different here."

Source: NSE publications and brochures

8

"To support its mission to be a force for good, the company created the Nu Skin Force for Good with the introduction of the company's Epoch line of ethnobotanical personal care products. Because Epoch products are derived from the ancient botanical wisdom of indigenous culture, the company wanted to find a way to "give something back" to these treasured communities. Funded by percentage of Epoch product sales — and donation from employees, distributors, and the cooperation — the Nu Skin Force for Good Foundation has contributed millions of dollars to worthy causes all across the globe".

Source: NSE publications, speech scripts, Nu Skin Newsletter

9

Related saying: "One person make a difference. One person, no matter where they live, can help preserve island ecosystems and cultures. (Paul Cox, Ph.D., Seacology & Brain Chemistry Labs Founder)

Source: Seacology Brochure

Related saying: "None of us may be to change the world all at once, working together, we can make a difference. We invite you to become a part of the team that is working to save our planet, one island at time."

Paul Cox, Ph.D., Seacology and The Brain Chemistry Labs Founder.

Dr. Paul Cox: Graduated Harvard University, one of the world's foremost doctors of ethnology and botany, former Dean of the College of Arts and Sciences at Brigham Young University, professor of the House of Bernadotte, winner of the "Goldman Environmental Award", which is known as the "Nobel Prize for the Environment," and a master of Japanese culture, haiku, and ukiyo-e, publisher of numerous papers and books, and founder of the Seacology Foundation Brain Chemistry Laboratory

Source: Seacology brochures, books, research papers, websites, and social media

11

"We never doubted we could find consumers because we wanted to use the products ourselves. And that was enough to get us past the experts and their advice."

Source: Nu Skin Newsletter & Brochure

Author's note: NSE quotes from the early days of the founding of the company used to emphasize the quality of the active ingredients, but the citation categories of the quotes soon expanded. They expanded from the narrow sense of "customers first" in the direct sales market to the broad sense of the social significance of the "social mission and responsibility of the manufacturing industry." In addition, as sales competition intensified, they came to be cited as quotes for standing out in terms of product quality. Today, product demonstrations demand sophisticated product introductions that appeal to the audience with tactful, beautiful wording and highly sensitive narration.

12

"Everywhere we go, we appeal to people committed to making something of value and to achieving their dreams. We see this in every country — people who rise, becoming great and amazing.

Source: NSE publications

13

"I remember wondering every day what tomorrow would bring. I remember talking to successful leaders — and telling them about our philosophy and approach — , tomorrow, we can find one more person who think like us."

Source: NSE publications

14

"1 percent commitment takes 99 percent thought."

Source: Lecture Notes

15

"Throughout Nu Skin's 20 years, you have embraced our new products, services and initiatives with unbridled passion, and you have been inspiring leaders to thousands."

Source: Speech at the Team Elite Monaco Trip 2004 (thank you speech at Team Elite Monaco Trip 2004)

16

"The work of Nourish the Children may be just 5% of our business, but 95% of it represents our way of life."

Source: Nu Skin Newsletter - speech script

17

"Since the beginning of our founding, we have been working to become a 'Force for Good' in the world. Nourish the Children gives malnourished and starving children a breath of life. There is nothing better than the work of Force for Good."

Source: Nu Skin Newsletter - speech script

18

"Strangely, the more we serve others, the bigger our company grows - and I want to grow it into a company with more than a billion dollars in sales. I want to make it the company with the most social contribution in the world."

Compiler Note: Already achieved.

Source: Nu Skin Newsletter - speech script

19

"I am a big believer that everybody has unusual, and certainly untapped, potential. The more people like that we can line up with their skill set and with their abilities, the more success we get to have."

Source: Nu Skin Newsletter - "Founder's Quotes" "This Month's Words" Leading to Success

20

"I think it's really critical to have your dream life in your mind so that you are constantly adjusting and designing your business in such a way to accomplish that because you could very easily be highly successful and not accomplish your lifestyle you really want to accomplish in your heart."

Source: NSE Publication, Nu Skin Newsletter - "Founder's Quotes" "This Month's Words" Leading to Success

21

"I am a big believer that everybody has unusual, certainly untapped, potential. The more people like that we can line up with their skill set and with their abilities, the more success we get to have."

Source: Orientation Materials, "AZ Quotes" - Blake Roney Quotes

22

"Everyone needs to know their own 'reason for doing business.' I know very clearly why I have a strong passion for this business. As I look at it, there are still tens of thousands, even hundreds of thousands, of people in the world who cannot realize their dreams because they lack only a little support. I believe that I can help them and lead them to success. That belief is the source of my passion and my 'reason for doing business.'"

Source: Orientation Materials, Nu Skin Newsletter

23

"The most important thing in the world is not 'where' you are, but in 'what direction' you are heading."

Source: Nu Skin Newsletter, Lecture Notes

24

"The secret to success is to find 10 friends and help them succeed. I sincerely think so."

Source: Nu Skin Newsletter, Lecture Notes

25

"It's hard for anyone to approach someone for the first time, especially at the beginning. I have also been treated coldly by people who are wary of others. What I learned from that experience is the importance of believing that I can make their lives better. If you believe so while talking to them, your positive feelings will be transmitted to them, and they will open up their hearts more often."

Source: Nu Skin Newsletter, Lecture Notes

26

"If you actually act, your fears will disappear. For example, if you are feeling uneasy about talking to people, go outside and actually talk to others. Then, it will be easier and easier to talk to them, and you will find that there is nothing to be afraid of. I was the same way, and if I slack off on acting for a month, the same unease is reborn. Therefore, the easiest way to avoid being trapped by unease is to acknowledge yourself as being uneasy and then continue to act."

Source: Nu Skin Newsletter, Lecture Notes, Founder's Quotes

27

"When you help more people, you find greater success. Through movements such as Nourish the Children, we become more and more active in helping others. This virtuous circle is created only when we have our 'desire to enrich the lives of others.' The act of 'helping others' is a gift from heaven."

Source: Nu Skin Newsletter, Lecture Notes, Founder's Quotes

28

Analogous saying: "They will be the people who give, who like to bring delight to other people, and therefore gain pleasure and satisfaction for themselves." (Walt Disney)

Source: AZ Quotes, Collection of Walt Disney Sayings

29

"The future is created today. It depends on what you do today. The future is not fixed, nor is it going to come by itself. The future will change in whatever way depending on what you do today. The future is not something you expect, but something you create now. You can change yourself and your future even if you can't change others and your past. Everything starts with one person. Everything starts today. Everything is decided by small differences."

Source: AZ Quotes, Lecture Notes

30

"If you surround yourself with people who are trying to build, who are all willing to build other people up, they build you up!"

Source: AZ Quotes, Orientation Materials

31

"When you interact with people who are willing to develop people, they will develop you."

Source: AZ Quotes, Orientation Materials

32

"It seems that those who succeed as distributors have a stronger desire to give to others than ordinary people. They want to do things that are not directly related to their business, like providing food to African children. But they understand the truth that doing something to improve another's life helps them grow their own business — and they're trying to show it to others too."

Source: AZ Quotes, Lecture Notes

33

"Sitting and thinking about fear is like sitting on the cold poolside and imagining how cold it would be when you first dive in. The fear grows greater and greater. When you actually jump in, you think, 'Hey? That wasn't that bad. I'm glad I did it. I should have jumped in an hour ago.'"

Source: Nu Skin Newsletter, Formula for Infinite Growth

34

"A good person is a person who enriches the lives of others."

Source: Nu Skin Newsletter, Lecture Notes

35

"Just having one person who is negative can negate the efforts of those who are positive. So, always keep away from negative people and avoid getting involved with them."

Source: Speech Script, Lecture Notes

36

"The Japanese people have not only built our past, but they are also the power to create our future."

Source: Speech Script, Lecture Notes

37

"I have met people who are excellent in posture and form. All people have huge potential, so they seem to have their hands in a special pool. If only everyone understood exactly where those are."

Source: Speech Script, Orientation Materials: The Success Formula

38

"If fears are just negative ideas, then for a moment, replace them with positive words and images. Take a break, write down some of your fears, and then write down what you are replacing them with."

Source: Speech Script, Orientation Materials: The Success Formula

39

"Please design a path to build your business, such as 'I will not sacrifice my family.' You must not lose your relationship with your partner, who is so important. You must not lose your friendship, faith, or important sense of values for money. Far from being unnecessary, it is a mistake. You lose them in exchange for success."

Source: Speech Script, Orientation Materials: The Success Formula

40

"Speaking to strangers is 'challenging' for all of us. Especially in the beginning. In my case, not only was the other person in a mood to accept me in a friendly way, they were even mistrustful. However, the more you continue to talk with the other person, the more you will think, 'If this person accepts me, I can enrich my life.' This will strengthen your position."

Source: Speech Script, Orientation Materials: The Success Formula

41

"Be careful to avoid the 'self-centered' type of people. Okay? Please avoid them. Please do not accept such people into your group. They will ruin the whole group."

Source: Speech Script, Orientation Materials: The Success Formula

42

"Speaking to strangers is 'challenging' for all of us. 'Today I will go and find who to help.' That is how we have built this business like magic. It is also a way which allows one to think 'This is nice. I like myself. I like what I do. I like the lifestyle of the Nu Skin family.' every night before bed."

Source: Speech Script, Orientation Materials: The Success Formula

43

"A good person is a person who is looking to help others."

Source: Speech Script, Orientation Materials: The Success Formula

44

"Hidden within each of us is the ability to do more with our lives. And it's up to us to make the decision to do it and then do it through Nu Skin as the powerful vehicle to it."

Source: NSE Publications, Orientation Materials

45

"MAKING A DIFFERENCE; I am amazed, awed, and humbled by what we have been able to accomplish ...by working together toward a common goal — to help each other fulfill our dreams and to act as a force for good throughout the world."

Source: NSE Publications, Lecture Notes

46

"Our pursuit to be the world's leading direct selling company has driven Nu Skin Enterprises since 1984 and continues to be a guiding force today. Our goal is to make every product superior in its category — differentiated products and implement novel and most of all to pay our distributors more in commissions than is paid out by any other direct selling company."

Source: Speech at the Team Elite Monaco trip 2004 (script of thank you speech at Team Elite Monaco trip 2004)

47

"The most important thing I do for myself is to maintain a positive attitude no matter what."

Source: Founder's Quotes, Orientation Notes

48

Analogous quote: "In everyone lies the potential to enrich their own life. Whether or not you can develop your skills through the wonderful opportunity of your Nu Skin business depends on your own decisions."

Source: Nu Skin Newsletter - "Founder's Quotes" "This Month's Words"
Leading to Success, Lecture Notes

49

"The reason Nu Skin is recognized as one of the best companies in the global Internet direct sales industry is that each of us is following the same path with one accord. That is also why we can pay more commission than other companies and why Force for Good can contribute to society, such as providing food aid to poor children. In other words, we are all working together as a team."

Source: Nu Skin Newsletter, Lecture Notes

50

"You must begin by enhancing your own abilities. If you do so, you will naturally be an example to others, and your advice will be more persuasive."

Source: Founder's Quotes, Lecture Notes

51

"It's a great opportunity to show the beauty of Nu Skin products when people say things like 'Your skin is beautiful,' 'You look young,' 'You're full of energy,' etc. When you talk about how you became appealing, people understand the reliability and quality of the product. They will also open their hearts to your explanations of business opportunities."

Source: Founder's Quotes, Lecture Notes

52

"Confidence in products and confidence in business opportunities are inseparable. These two are closely linked."

Source: Founder's Quotes, Speech Script

53

"You must not think, 'I still do not have enough to give to others. I will give when I am richer.' You do not give because you have wealth, but rather wealth arises because you give. What's more, giving is a very pleasant act. Why should we hesitate to give? Start with what you can do now, and enlarge your wealth and the joy you give at the same time."

Source: Founder's Quotes, Orientation Materials

54

"We often see people confronting each other because of differences in opinion. We do not want such things at Nu Skin. We work towards the same goals, like Force for Good, but we do not have to take the same approach when doing business. If someone else is using a different method, listen to them, and if you also want to try it, then you should incorporate it into your business. On the other hand, if you do not think that it suits you, you should not incorporate it. Therefore, let's think simply about whether it suits us or not, rather than confronting each other with worries, and progress forward."

Source: Founder's Quotes, Orientation Materials

55

"The experience of overcoming something opens up our potential."

Source: Nu Skin Newsletter, Lecture Notes

56

"As you gain greater success, you will have many opportunities to make social returns. Do not miss such opportunities, and continue the practice of giving to others, though it may be only small things at first. Because the more you give to others, the more quickly your success will accelerate. And the stronger your spirit of compassion and sharing, the more zeal you will have for enriching the world and moving towards a Force for Good."

Source: Founder's Quotes, Orientation Materials

57

"I have been exposed to many success stories, and I have realized that not only does this business dramatically change the lives of individuals and their families, it also changes society as a whole. This business is growing hugely. The number of people who are given dreams and hopes by our business opportunities and who not only enrich their lives but also contribute to society as a Force for Good is greater than we can imagine. As one of those who provide business opportunities, this situation fills my heart with joy and gratitude."

Source: Founder's Quotes, Orientation Materials

58

"To be successful in business, you need to get rid of useless old habits, and develop habits that are useful to you. Habits arise from repetition, but bad habits are easy to acquire, while good ones are difficult to acquire. But once good habits are acquired, they clarify our sense of existence and bring us greater satisfaction and feelings of accomplishment."

Source: Founder's Quotes, Orientation Materials

59

"When you're distracted by the difficulties that block you, the people who want to criticize others, the anxieties, these negative factors, you cannot focus on the exciting and joyful journey of your Nu Skin Business, and success becomes doubtful. And if you do not help others as you were helped, you still will not be able to succeed. In other words, the foundation of this business is 'being positive' and 'helping others.'"

Source: Founder's Quotes, Orientation Materials

60

"Planning is essential to success. Successful people get through a lot of work as if they are using all 24 hours of the day and produce many results. They assign priorities to their work and work in a balanced manner. They do not put things off and then panic later or get into a situation where they work on several projects but cannot finish even one. This is because they are plan-oriented and have fully developed the habit of managing their schedule."

Source: Founder's Quotes, Orientation Materials

61

"Once you decide to take action, it is your responsibility to make your dream come true. No one else will do it for you. Nobody else will say, 'Oh, this is your dream.' It cannot happen. You achieve it by your own actions. If you want it, you must create it yourself."

Source: Founder's Quotes, Orientation Materials

62

"It can be said that life is full of problems, or it can be said that life is full of wonderful blessings. It all depends on what side you see. Some people find difficulties every time they have a chance, while others find chances every time they have a difficulty. So, which are you?"

Source: Founder's Quotes, Orientation Materials

63

"The more you grow, the more you give back to society. The more you improve, the better your leader qualities will be. In the end, continuing to grow will lead to your own happiness."

Source: Founder's Quotes, Orientation Materials

64

"If you feel like you are stuck at your current level and you really want to take it to the next level, if you want to develop further for yourself, please take action. It's for you."

Source: Founder's Quotes, Orientation Materials

65

"We hear from everyone that the greatest challenge in work is to get people to stop worrying. We are born with a number of fears. Regardless of the extent of their impact, whether you lose to those fears or overcome them depends on your choice."

Source: Founder's Quotes, Orientation Materials

66

"This company enables people to improve their own abilities to lead, communicate, and navigate life's waters".

Source: NSE Publications, Orientation Materials

67

Analogous saying: "Outstanding leadership and teamwork are the must-win conditions in all competitions." (Unable to identify founder)

Source: NSE Publications, Orientation Materials

68

"UNLIMITED POTENTIAL; I continued to be impressed by the overall quality and elegance of our organization. Brilliant minds and world class entrepreneurs have been attracted to the unlimited potential — to the exceptional integrity of our highly innovative and scientifically formulated products. To support the efforts of our dynamic distributor forces, we have developed a solid corporate infrastructure that allows our distributors to bring — to people across the glove — , but one of the biggest companies in the world."

Source: NSE Publications, Orientation Materials

69

"Adages such as 'belief without action is meaningless' or 'belief alone is not enough' are truths common to almost every culture. Such adages teach us, 'Rather than shutting yourself in your home, act according to your own convictions. If you do not, you will never succeed.'"

Source: Nu Skin Newsletter, Orientation Materials

70

"I know people who make scary amounts of money and lead a wild life that makes me want to cover my eyes. For me, they are far from successful people. Conversely, others have a moderate income, but they are rich in creativity, strive to be of service to others, and live a life filled with joy. To me, they are successful people. Your amount of income has nothing to do with success."

Source: Founder's Quotes, Orientation Materials

71

"If you started to work to buy a boat because your neighbor bought one, even if you continued to get up early in the morning every day to do work that you didn't like, you could not continue this for a long time. On the other hand, if your beloved son wouldn't be able to go to college if you didn't manage to somehow save for school expenses, you would have endless motivation in your heart. Being fully aware of the reason why you work serves as a spring of motivation."

Source: Founder's Quotes, Orientation Materials

72

"To be successful, you need to know what you want. I believe that you are of high worth and that you will gain things equivalent to that worth. If you want something from the bottom of your heart, you will actually be able to get it."

Source: Founder's Quotes, Orientation Materials

73

"To have a purpose in life. That is, to discover something that is worth your best effort. If you can do that, you can achieve far greater results than material rewards.

Source: Founder's Quotes, Orientation Materials

74

"Courage is not the lack of fear. Courage is doing what you should do despite your unease."

Source: Founder's Quotes, Orientation Materials

75

"Most people hesitate to act for psychological reasons, not physical reasons. Through successful experiences of taking chances and achieving something, people can be freed from such fear and gain a strong spiritual strength. Even those who shake in fear while 'frightened to death' can smile from their hearts, saying, 'I can do it,' if they have had successful experiences."

Source: Founder's Quotes, Orientation Materials

76`

"The popular measures of money, property, and title have little to do with success. I hope that people who try their hands at Nu Skin businesses do not think 'I am not a success because I do not make a lot of money.' If you work according to your values and find joy in your deeds, you are a successful person. People who are lonely and have money are not successful, because they have sacrificed their families and friends to make money. This is the tragedy of an unbalanced life, and it is failure."

Source: Founder's Quotes, Orientation Materials

77

"I have been in a bad spot before, so I understand that sales is the hardest job. Surely there are some who, every time they wake up, ask themselves 'How can I go sell that product today?' or 'Why am I going through such effort to undergo such bad experiences?' Some people will leave this business because they cannot stand the pain of selling. I would like to say to such people: 'We work to make the people we meet happier than before.'"

Source: Founder's Quotes

78

"We have conducted a number of surveys over the years to try to identify the characteristics of successful people. However, we found little in common in terms of academic background, work background, accomplishments, home country, social status, and individual characteristics. Despite that, there is one thing we learned. What successful people have in common is their strong 'will to succeed.'"

Source: Founder's Quotes

79

"All of us have the ability to learn new things, and this exciting ability doesn't disappear until we die. One of the keys to success is to make the most of this learning ability. There are people who say, "I don't have the skills to succeed" when they come across this business. I reply, 'So what? You obviously would not have the skills at this point.' Even brain surgeons could not operate on brains on the first day of their enrollment in medical school. Any skill can be acquired after learning."

Source: Founder's Quotes, Orientation Materials

80

"Don't be afraid of new challenges because you are 'not used to it yet.' If you dare to challenge yourself, you will grow as a human being. And from that growth, amazing results are born."

Source: Founder's Quotes, Orientation Materials

81

Analogous adage: "You must not fear engaging in new things. Because nobody knows everything about them. Just by engaging with them, you will achieve great work, and that will also serve as your personal growth."

Source: Speech Script, Orientation Materials: The Success Formula

82

"There are three ways to motivate people. The first is 'unease.' This is useful in the short term, but the effect does not last long. The second is 'rewards.' If one can receive a reward, the results improve somewhat. However, rewards alone do not give us the strength to overcome the difficulties we face in life. The third is 'purpose.' Only 'purpose' gives us a clear vision to overcome difficulties and motivation to persist."

Source: Founder's Quotes

83

Analogous idiom: "In order for one to learn the important lessons of life, one must first overcome a fear each day." (Ralph Emerson: American philosopher)

Source: Brochure excerpt

84

Analogous immortal saying: "When it comes to superficial things, you may follow the world. However, when it comes to essential things, firmly follow your own beliefs." (Thomas Jefferson: Third President of the United States)

Source: Idiom and saying dictionary

85

"Everyday, take the action 'giving to others.' That includes giving kind words of encouragement to those who are stuck in this work and providing food to starving children whose lives are threatened. These actions contribute to the world beyond your imagination. And they give you unbelievable power as well."

Source: Founder's Quotes

86

"Don't lose your attitude of learning. The words 'Life ends when we give up on learning' are true. Learning requires an attitude of always checking your work. When you give a presentation, be sure to take some time to reflect on, 'What went well, and what should I improve?' If a six-month-old presentation is not better than today's presentation, then that person is not learning. That person has lost the greatest value that this business has to offer, that is, to improve one's skills and grow as a human being. Please continue to be a learner."

Source: Founder's Quotes, Orientation Materials

87

Related quote: "We decided a long time ago that if we wanted to achieve results never before accomplished, we must expect to employ methods never before attempted."

Source: NSE Publications, Orientation Materials

88

Related quote: "Throughout history, sailors have heard the refrain, — "It can't be done." From sailing around the presumably flat world to finding the fabled Northwest Passage to China, those who lack vision have been proven wrong time and time again."

Source: NSE publications

89

"Moms and dads, your sons need you to support them now as passionately as ever you have in the past when they have been about lesser things like badges and pins."

Source: Website

90

"The power of humans is very intriguing to me. That is because no one has criteria. No one knows how much we can achieve. We have tools that can do more than we understand. There is no room for doubt that you all can go farther, rise higher, and do more than you have believed until now."

Source: Speech Script, Orientation Materials: The Success Formula

91

"Learn to bravely tackle things that surprise people, live on, progress forward, and try other things. You should have a heart that says 'This does not mean that I should not tackle something while I am frightened of it. And it definitely does not mean that I cannot do anything.'"

Source: Speech Script, Orientation Materials: The Success Formula

92

"If someone is fighting over a difference in values, there is something I want to say. I want to say 'Order is not achieved by extraordinary values.' This is a social, intellectual, and sincere manner of speaking. Everyone has unfathomable value."

Source: Speech Script, Orientation Materials: The Success Formula

93

"In group activities and sports team play, there is an important lesson that it is more important to think about 'the whole' than 'the total.' We need to work together. It is only when each one of us collaborates with the other members that we can move forward."

Source: Speech Script, Orientation Materials: The Success Formula

94

"The path to perfecting human abilities has a good side in that we can emulate others. Always be a cheerful, lively, positive-thinking, and hopeful person. However, I still agree with Blake Roney's position that 'If there is someone who we cannot welcome, we should distance ourselves.'"

Source: Speech Script, Orientation Materials: The Success Formula

95

"Years ago, Blake and I discussed 'How rich is rich?' The two of us tried our hands at calculating and reached a certain number. You wanted to ask one of us for it now, didn't you? The two of us have reached different values, but 'rich' is not measurable by numbers. Riches are not money, assets, appealing toys, or an environment overflowing with a lifestyle, but rather an inner sensibility and useful contributions to life. Sometimes a positive life means what you have stored up. That is what 'rich' is."

Source: Speech Script, Orientation Materials: The Success Formula

96

"Just like the single stone that creates a ripple effect across the water, the good work of our distributors is extending outward and creating a wave of hope for people throughout the world."

Source: NSE publications

97

"While it is important for a sailboat racing team to identify and recruit the most talented crew members possible, it is just as important — perhaps even more so — to retain them. It is far more challenging to replace lost team members than it is to keep them in the first place."

Source: NSE publications

98

"When started, I don't know how many times people asked "Why are you called Nu Skin International?" But that was always the plan — we always knew we' have global appeal."

Source: NSE publications

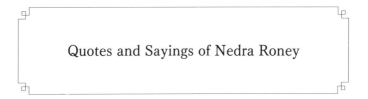

Quotes and Sayings of Nedra Roney

99

"Our philosophy has always been 'all of the good, none of the bad.'"

Source: Founder's Quotes, Orientation Materials

100

"All of Good, None of Bad" (Nedra Roney 1958 - 2021)

Source: Nu Skin Newsletter, Speech Script, Orientation Materials

101

"Nourish the Children is an initiative that applies business principals to address the problem of children hunger in a sustainable manner."

Source: NSE Publications, Websites, Orientation Materials

102

Related quote: "I hope you will continue to find satisfaction as you make a difference in the lives of the people of Malawi —" (Gary Garrette; Managing Director, Nu Skin Force for Good Foundation)

Source: "2010-2013Photo book of SAFI (School of Agriculture for Family Independence) at Mtalimanja Village, Malawi"

103

"Strong leadership and reliable support system are essential ingredients in every successful sailing competition. Strong leaders set the course for others to follow while a reliable support system ensures that the team has everything it needs to complete its journey. Together, these two elements make a team unstoppable."

Source: NSE publications

104

"Positioned to offer support or aid" — As they journey from familiar place to faraway lands, global travelers continued to find a sense of home in a culture where helping others is the key to personal successes."

Source: NSE publications

105

"Alongside — Charting a course across unknown waters is a journey fraught with challenges, and uncertainties, but it can also be a journey filled with wonder and exhilaration. Those who embark on such journey must be willing to keep their eyes focused on the horizon, to read the winds of change, to take advantage of new opportunities, and to develop a strong framework of support and inspiration with those who work beside them."

Source: NSE publications

106

"As boats get bigger, the stresses from wind and waves increase in direct proportion. The wise sailor understands the need for having a well-designed boat. Outfitted with quality sails and hardware, it must be built to last. The middle of the ocean — days or even weeks away from help — is not the place to find out that standards were not high enough."

Source: NSE publications

107

"The dream of creating a company to improve lives has become a reality. This dream was forged by noble pioneers on a quest for freedom. Today, the dream reaches around the globe and offers people the opportunity to live better, longer — to navigate their own destinies; not only to provide for their children, but to be there —."

Source: NSE publications

108

"JOURNEY SPEAKS OF ANTICIPATION — beginnings, points of departure, possibilities, potential. A journey conveys motion — momentum, realization, potential. A journey tells the story of realization, destinations, goals, future ventures, uncharted territories. NU SKIN ENTERPRISES IS THE STORY OF A JOURNEY — A CONTINUING JOURNEY."

Source: NSE publications

109

"Life's journey is never linear. By its very nature, life is dynamic and diverse, it is subject to change. And while the destination may be clearly envisioned and expectations well defined, one discovers that reality often refuses to adhere to even the most carefully contemplated course. Indeed, the hallmark of successful journey is that events never meet expectations, but instead exceed them every time."

Source: NSE publications

110

Analogous saying: "Twenty years from now, you will be more disappointed by the things you didn't do than by the ones you did do. So, throw off the bowlines. Sail away from the safe harbor. Catch the trade wind in your sails. Explore. Dream. Discover." (Mark Twain)

Source: NSE publications

111

"Ultimately, taking the first step in a voyage across unknown waters requires commitment, focus and faith. Commitment to the task at hand during each stage of the journey. Focus on what's most important. And faith in one's own abilities to navigate rough waters."

Source: NSE publications

112

Analogous adage: "Our most successful leaders are people who put other people first... in the long run, that's exactly what makes them successful."

Source: Nu Skin Newsletter

113

"If your fear is talking to people, then go out and talk to people. You will find it just keeps getting easier and there's really nothing to be afraid of. However, I can tell you that if I stop for a month, It starts to seem scary again. So, the easiest way to fend off fear is to attack it, embrace it."

Source: Nu Skin website - "Founder's Quotes" "This Month's Words"
       Leading to Success

114

Analogous quote: "Success cannot be enjoyed alone. Tell others about your success. If you do, you can celebrate your success with everyone." (Troy Dunn: NSE executive)

Source: Nu Skin Newsletter

115

Related quote: "Vita Meal factory owner and operator
— Napoleon Dzombe is visionary behind the School of
Agriculture for Family Independence (SAFI). — Vita
Meal is delicious. — I am so thankful to be part of this
most amazing effort to 'Nourish the Children' — Now I
can see that we are making a difference." (The author
unknown)

Source: NSE Global Destination Report

116

"The sense of satisfaction that you have achieved your
goals opens a new door to life. Beyond the door is a
wonderful future that you do not know yet." (Tamako
Kishimoto: NS Team Elite)

117

"By adding up small challenges one by one, we learn the joy and fun of overcoming." (Tamako Kishimoto: NS Team Elite)

118

"I want to challenge myself on how much I can serve people until I'm 100 years old — When I'm 100 years old, I want to talk about my dreams for 120 years old." (Tamako Kishimoto: NS Team Elite)

119

"To the 100-year-old me who has the power to show miracles, shine brightly and wait for me." (Tamako Kishimoto: NS Team Elite)

120

Example of rhythmic poem: "Now, now, in the time called now, there is no now, in the time called now, now has already gone." (author unknown)

Source: Edo period books, NSE Orientation Materials

121

"Where there is a will, there is a way. Where there is no will, there is no way. All failure is a lack of man's will." (Yozan Uesugi: Lord of the Yonezawa Domain)

Source: Edo period books, NSE Orientation Materials

122

"My Nu Skin business has taught me how to live a quality life." (Tamako Kishimoto: NS Team Elite)

123

"Nothing Happens Without a Dream." (Masayuki Kishimoto: NS Team Elite)

Source: "Working at Home" Success Magazine

Afterword

Why has Nu Skin rapidly grown into a leading company in the global online direct sales industry in the short period of its founder's lifetime? My main motivation for editing this book was to find the answer.

I wanted to start searching for answers from the founders' sayings and quotes. In addition to 113 quotes from the founders, 10 distributor-related quotes were included in this book. There are many other things that have not been searched, scrutinized, or publicized yet.

After editing, I was convinced that Nu Skin was meant to succeed, and so it did. My hypothesis in the "Introduction" of this book was confirmed.

Even before the founding of the company in 1984, the founders had fostered in their hearts a life philosophy that moved people's hearts and the "mission and responsibility of the company."

In other words, they had been nurturing their own hearts since before the company was founded. Their hearts were truly the spirit of "Force for Good."

The extraordinary success of Nu Skin may be said to be the "sustainable success" of the "founders' hearts."

The question now is whether they can sustain their brilliant success. The question is whether the next generation of company management and leading distributors can "move people's hearts." We cannot sustain "sustainable success" simply by properly understanding market trends and using cutting-edge digital technology.

The recorded 123 quotes, adages, and sayings are a bit different from the usual. I chose to write them in simple words to make them easy for anyone to understand, in prose rather than poetry.

However, their essential meaning is not compromised at all. Rather, the prose style of writing forms an extract and absorbs into the human mind. The gallant spirit of "Force for Good" is reminiscent of poets' 'sincere' personality, leading me to bow my head instinctively.

The founder and president Blake Roney reminisced that "Strangely enough, our company has developed further the more we have served others." I thought this a very humble way to say it. My mind was particularly struck by this saying that the joy of being able to serve others and contribute to society is the greatest blessing in life.

While editing this book, I was also very happy to form bonds to the Nu Skin spirit together with other distributors of the same intent. On the other hand, I found words that "move people's hearts" and felt frustrated that I could not express them well. I felt that I had to narrow the gap between the thoughts my heart wants to express and my writing abilities.

The founders of NSE are committed to communicating the sayings and adages from all times and places that our predecessors have used as "mottos" to the masses in simple words while aligning them the knowledge that they have polished. That thoughtfulness touches the heartstrings of the listener.

There are also analogous sayings. "To move a person, you have to move the person's heart" (Dale Carnegie) Moving a person's heart moves their body. When the bodies move, society moves. The hearts and bodies of people are interlocked and move the world. In other words, our hearts move toward the ultimate desire of humankind, "lasting world peace."

The nationalistic hearts are absorbed by globalist hearts. Also, the spirit of nationalism is absorbed by the spirit of universal co-prosperity. This kind of movement of the heart can be called the elevation of the human heart. In other words, historical events, idioms, adages, sayings, and quotes from all times and places can be called "world heritage of the hearts of all mankind."

Recently, I often think this: What if authoritarian powers who have committed grave genocide crimes, such as the Hitler, Tojo, Mussolini, Pol Pot, Nimeiri, Stalin, Min Aung Hlaing, and Putin governments, had even a little reverence for this "world heritage of the hearts of all mankind"? Surely, the "modern human history of violence" would have been avoided. I think so with my head, I lament with my heart, and I try to act with my body.

I have a suggestion. Add historical events, idioms, adages, sayings, and quotes from all times and places as world heritage of the heart to the mandatory curriculum for school education on a global scale. This is because I believe that this will greatly contribute to increasing the power to bring about lasting world peace.

People carefully select words while thinking with words. However, there are times when there are no words even in the dictionary. This must be the limit of human language. It may exist in insect language. Then, I fall into the quandary of "What is this fogginess called?" However, I think that the sayings and adages of all times and places have clues to answer such problems. Furthermore, the various forms of human-made barriers are not present in sayings and adages. They all contribute to the health of global society.

"Movement of the heart" is not something that waits, but something that moves. That is to say, universal education is the driving force. In other words, I believe that there is value in putting collections of adages and sayings from all times and places in a shared textbook for global education.

I am optimistic that a more elevated and healthier world order will be created when every global citizen respects the world heritage of the heart even more deeply. This is because optimism always surpasses pessimism. Therefore, we will make a global peaceful civilization sustainable.

In today's rapidly growing text of various genres, texts such as historical events, idioms, adages, sayings, and quotes are relatively small in terms of controversy (inviting conflict). The contradictions in dogma (doctrinal contradictions) between monotheism and polytheism, between denominations and sects, as has happened in the global religious world, will less readily arise. There are no points of controversy like those causing the so-called "world religious wars." Therefore, even if the approval of an obligatory textbook common to all mankind is proposed, it will not cause heated conflict.

The joy of contributions to society that accomplish the

philanthropy of "Force for Good" around the world will stimulate people's positive thinking and lead to the establishment of public order and morals for global civil society. As far as physical and material social contributions, they can be done by AI robots and digital transformation (DX).

The act of being pleased and respected by others moves people's hearts and elevates their motives for action. Therefore, many eternal sayings have been created, such as "the world moves when the human heart moves."

Sayings and adages from all times and places help to reform people's consciousness. They contribute to the purification and elevation of human society.

When the consciousness of sovereign states can be upgraded to the consciousness of a global state, the reform of the collective consciousness of one world and one humankind is advanced. Such "movement of the heart" moves the world, makes people realize that borders are unnecessary, and contributes to developing a sense of aversion to world wars.

In recent years, a pandemic named human heart putrefaction has been rampant, and the promotion of education that creates "antibodies in the human heart" is a pressing issue. The warning bells of the health crisis on Earth, the small planet that is the home of all life, do not stop ringing.

Lastly, I would like to add three "eternal sayings" that I have made my "mottos." "Motto" means a book of lifelong teaching.

"There is no better way to learn than to experience yourself." (Einstein)

Academic learning and experiential learning. The learning effect of the latter is more practical and more sustainable. Of course, we must not forget that the synergy between the two produces a multiplication effect.

When people are happy with their own sensibilities about their own learning outcomes, the human perspective expands on a global scale. The globalization of the physical and spiritual is a shortcut to lasting peace.

Anyone can become an expert when they can make the things they like sustainable. There is also a saying left by our predecessors, "What one likes, one will do well." We feel "worth in doing" and "worth in living" in the things we like. We also come to understand that the evolution of civilization accelerates when the number of experts increases. Also, the emotion of feeling happy promotes the secretion of active hormones in the body.

"It is more dangerous that there is someone overlooking evil than there being someone influenced by evil." (Einstein)

In life, we are often forced to make a difficult choice between two evils. There are many people who are aware of evil and yet become infected with it, and also people who are aware of it but overlook it. Compared with the former, the latter are cowardly and ugly people. If anyone yearns for a comfortable group society, they must take a bold stand against their companions who do bad and admonish them on good and evil.

"Imagination is more important than knowledge. For knowledge is limited, whereas imagination embraces the entire world, stimulating progress, giving birth to evolution." (Einstein) The world needs 10,000 prospective critics of the future more than 100 million retrospective critics of the past. The past cannot create the future, but the present can create the future. In other words, critics who can imagine a future outlook are more valuable.

However, it is said that even scientific forecasts of the future are 80% inaccurate. Nevertheless, future development will never stop. This is because one can acquire the imagination to shift today's suffering to tomorrow's joy.

Modern people who are improving their imagination can realize their ideals with their imagination. The realization of the ideal can be accelerated by the learning results of "historical events, idioms, adages, and sayings." This is why I am driven by the impulse of wanting to repeatedly emphasize the value of a mandatory curriculum in school education.

Man, who governs at the pinnacle of the living world, continues to evolve reliably and at an accelerated pace. Without a doubt, each step is approaching lasting world peace. When I imagine the future world in half a century, my heart is elated. Human beings will soon arrive at the end of the line, called "Lasting World Peace Station."

I am so pleased that the spirit of "Force For Good," which existed in the Nu Skin founders' hearts, is rapidly multiplying within independent distributors who realize that it is the essence of corporate philosophy. In other words, the corporate philosophy of "moving people's hearts" is becoming firmly established. People's passionate thoughts and the dream of sustainability will certainly become a reality.

Acknowledgments

I dedicate this book to my beloved wife, Tamako, who has been by my side for more than 60 years, and to my irreplaceable NSE comrades who are connected by the same dream.

Major References

Nihon Seisho Kankokai *"New Japanese Translation Large Bible,"* Word of Life, 2004.

Kazuo Inamori, *"Kazuo Inamori Daily Words,"* Chichi Publishing, 2021.

Yutaka Niihara, *"The life can find happiness,"* Sunmark Publishing, 2012.

Norihiko Hanada, *"Signs of the Times,"* Fukuinsha, 2021.

Ellen G. White, *"Patriarchs and Prophets,"* Fukuinsha, 2008.

D. H. Carnegie, edited by Dorothy Carnegie, Translated by Yasushi Kamishima,

"Dale Carnegie's Scrapbook", Sogensha, 2010.

D. H. Carnegie, translated by Hiroshi Yamaguchi, *"How to Win Friends and Influence People,"* Sogensha, 2016.

D. H. Carnegie, translated by Akira Kayama, *"How to Stop Worrying and Start Living,"* Sogensha, 2016.

Franklin Covey Japan: *"Quotes and Quips for living the '7 Habits,'"* King Bear Publishing, 2004.

Kanenori Masui, *"Dictionary of Sayings, Adages, and Idioms,"* Minerva Shobo, 2016.

Sanseido Editing, *"Idioms at a Glance"* Sanseido, 1999.

Hiroshi Ouchi & Janet Ouchi, *"Inspiring Quotations from Around the World,"* Kodansha Bilingual Book, 2000.

Sanseido Edition, *"Historical Event, Idiom, and Common Expression Dictionary"*, Sanseido, 2004. Masamizu Tokita, *"Iwanami Idiom Dictionary,"* Iwanami Shoten, 2000.

"World Sayings with Small Idiom Dictionary," Nagaoka Shoten, 1981.

"Quotations from Chairman Mao Tse-tung," Gaiko Shuppansha, 1966. (*Little Red Book)

Mary Kawena "PUKUI," OHANA , mutual publishing, 2003.

Nu Skin Enterprises, Inc., *"'Journey' the first 20 years of Nu Skin Enterprises,"* Graphic Art Center, 2004.

Nu Skin Force for Good Foundation, "The School of Agriculture for family independence at Mtalimanja Village, Malawi 2012 - 2013",

Paul Alan Cox, Michael J. Balick "Plants, People, and Culture", Scientific American Library, Division of HPHLP, 1996.

Author Profile

Masayuki Kishimoto

Living in Los Angeles

1934	Born in September
1957	Graduated from the Department of English Literature, The University of the Ryukyus
1961	Invited to the United States as a Fulbright Program student
1963	Obtained a master's degree from the University of Maryland
1965	Joined Japan Airlines and worked for 25 years thereafter
1997	Former Director of the National Tropical Botanical Garden (United States National Tropical Botanical Garden)
1998	Current Director of the Seacology Foundation (USA)
1999	Founded KFI Kishimoto Family International (USA: Seattle)
2003	Former Director of the Institute for EthnoMedicine (USA - founded by Dr. Paul Cox)
2007	Founded Kishimoto Family Foundation (USA). Contributed a total of 400 million yen to trade projects and about 700 million yen to university endowments (bequest funds) (amount totaled by tax management company)
2009	Onward Supported 22 families to study on exchange at "Mtalimanja Agriculture School for Family Independence (ASAFI)" in Malawi, Africa
2016	Established the "Kishimoto Bequest Fund" at his alma mater, the University of the Ryukyus Received an honorary doctorate from the University of the Ryukyus Served as the Director of the National Tropical Botanical Garden in Hawaii (Curator: Dr. Paul Cox), the Seacology Nature Conservation Organization, and the Institute for EthnoMedicine (founded by Dr. Paul Cox), and visited 20 countries around the world

Analects of the Founders' Quotes, Sayings, & Other Heartfelt Words

2023年5月15日　初版第1刷発行

著　者　Masayuki Kishimoto
発行者　瓜谷 綱延
発行所　株式会社文芸社
　　　　〒160-0022　東京都新宿区新宿1−10−1
　　　　　　　　電話 03-5369-3060（代表）
　　　　　　　　　　　03-5369-2299（販売）

印刷所　株式会社フクイン

ISBN978-4-286-24363-4